THE POWER OF FILIPINO SMILE.

Informal lived education and joy: 2006- 2017 (1st edition).

SAUT-MTWARA.

Recommended Citation,

Bago Adam, The Power of Filipino Smile, Lexington, KY: USA, Create space, 2018

Contact: mbaghopori@yahoo.com

INSIDE:.

ACKNOWLEDGEMENT

This work would not have been possible without the selfless love, commitment and generosity of the following people: The parents who offered the researcher to the Lord as a missionary priest. The congregation of the Holy Spirit which sent the researcher to the Philippines to work as a missionary. Province of Tanzania for allowing and supporting the researcher in different ways to study and eventually to learn more. Superior of Spiritan Philippines **Fr. Illah Agbne Cssp**, for his selfless support and encouragement. Parishioners of Digkilaan, for accepting the researcher to serve them as an assistant priest and Parish Priest for more than seven years. The Resurrection of the Lord Chinese-Filipino Parishners for their care, love and support in different ways. **Dr. Florami B. Dadole** for her encouragement. Program Instructional Managers who worked for more than seven years to make a difference in different groups but also for teaching me different ways of learning Filipino culture: **Mary Jane C. Capadiso, Juvy Siarza, Adrian Canoy, Michael Tingcan and Annalie Tucalo. Others are: Najiha Sumagayan, Noranie Cabugatan,Rosel Cabasag, Darling Conog, Ivy Bacalso,Mary Jane Katuran, Emelda and late Escala;** Maryknoll Institute of Language and Culture which taught the writer Filipino culture.

The DepEd Iligan, especially Schools Division **Superintendent Randolf B. Tortola, CESO VI** and Coordinators of Alternative Learning System (ALS) especially **Ma'am May, Rhodelia and Dr. Ruth. Others are Sr. Perez, Tingcan** and all ALS members of Iligan for their collaboration with the researcher to make a difference.

MSU IIT for training many women to get out of poverty through livelihood programs. **McDonnell Foundation** for the support of the program since it began. All friends from different religions and groups but especially **Bingle, Flora and Jonny. Holcim, Petronas, Ivory Printing & Publishing House.** **St. Michael's College** where the researcher took some units to allow him do the master's and doctorate degree programs and Xavier University for accepting the researcher to learn more about the Filipino culture. **Iligan Medical College** where the author taught. Unmentioned people and groups whom due to the limited of space and memory, the researcher failed to include here, know that God has mentioned you in His Kingdom. Most of all, to GOD ALMIGHTY, the source of man's wisdom, power, counsel and all understanding. All knowledge and talents shared to all forgotten communities belong to HIM. The Glory, Kingdom, Honor and praises belong to HIM forever and ever. ad majorem Dei gloriam-Amen

FOREWARD.

Keeping a positive attitude about the people, the culture and the challenges will always open the door of joy and fulfillment in the missionary life. We saw that in the beautiful mission story and experience of Fr. Adam Bago in the Philippines in the last 11 years.

Coming from a very different culture in far away Tanzania, Fr. Adam was able to create a web of love, joy and fulfillment through openness and dedication to the welfare of other people. It has been the mark of the Spiritan missionary life to be always available to the people we serve, but Fr. Adam went beyond availability to creativity in making the lives of so many poor farmers better in the Philippines.

In 2008, Fr. Adam took up one of the most difficult parishes in the Diocese of Iligan, Digkilaan. He planted his heart to the people and endured all the difficulties with joy and love. Working among Muslims, Lumads and Christians; Fr. Adam became a man of dialogue; he became the bridge for peace in the midst of Chaos that he found himself. Digkilaan Parish comprises of Mainit, Rogongon, Kalilangan, Panorogangan, Lemonsudan, santa Cruz and many other hinter land barangays. These are the most dangerous terrain of Iligan city as it is the home of some of the notorious rebels; MILF, NPA and the other groups.

Serving in Digkilaan parish brings you face to face with all kinds of reality. You have to trek for more than four hours on foot to go for masses in more than 30 chapels. There are chapels that no motor can enter, you have no choice than to work. One of the remotest of these Chapels is Binasan, Bucana, Kapistahan, Pinatagan, Sumagaysay, etc. Fr. Adam fell in love with all of these hurdles and served the people with joy. In 2013, Fr. Adam lunched a program called, 'We are Mad'; the MAD means; 'MAKING A DIFFERENCE'. Through this program, Fr. Adam advocated for the needs of the poorest of the poor. Through his constant efforts and visits to the department of Education, he insisted on the need to start a school at Binasan even though the place looks like the end of the world. He convinced the department of education and let the delegation to Binasan. He became the link between the lumads and the government. Today, his dream in Binasan has long been realized. Many Children are now going to school in Binasan. After the typoon Sendong in 2011, Fr. Adam began teaching children who were displaced and evacuated into the parish, he later founded a school to help the children. After building more than 300 temporary shelter for Christians, Muslims and lumads at the different parts of the mountain, he took a humanitarian step in creating livelihood to many typhoon victims.

One of the exceptional steps of Fr. Adam was that he decided to build 4 mosques for Muslims who had no place to pray after their mosque was destroyed by the flood. He created a sporting event called; play for peace. Muslims, Christians and lumad were organized together to play for peace. These events were great and transformative.

In this simple but book, Fr. Adam has captured the Joy of the Filipino; a people so blessed with a powerful attitude to life. Only the Filipino can still afford to smile even when he or she is under the storm. A Loving and easy going people, simple and beautiful inside out. Keep Smiling, 'do not allow the world to change your smile, but you rather change the world with your smile.'

Fr. Adam is back to Tanzania at this time for another journey of missionary life. May the Holy Spirit continue to guide and may the lovely memories of this beautiful country which you have now continue to inspire you every where you go.

God Bless

Rev. Fr. Illah Leo Agbene, CSSp

Superior, Spiritan Missionaries, Philippines.

DIFFERENT TASTE.

People look at one thing but come up with different interpretations.

People visit many countries and come out with different impressions.

People taste vinegar but give a different results. As what was said about oriental three great Philosophers: K'ung fu-tzu, Buddha and Laozi. These three men gathered around a vat of vinegar.
Each dipped a digit in then touched it to his tongue.
To K'ung Fu-tzu, the taste was sour; to Gautama Buddha, the taste was bitter; to Laozi, the taste was sweet. People may wonder why? Well, all is done in our mind.

According to the writer Philippines is his second home. Most of the times he forgot that he was a foreigner. He loves the country so much that as he has left that beautiful country, he thought it was good to send to the world a written work which someone could read and understand some few things and of course smile! This work is not covering every village or every tribe, neither does it cover every event in life or political discussion but rather it is based on the joy lived in the Philippines, the smile.

WHAT IS A SMILE?

A **smile** is a facial expression formed primarily by flexing the **muscles** at the sides of the **mouth**.

It is an expression
denoting pleasure, sociability, happiness, joy or amusement.

There are many divisions of smiles but the Health and Fitness May 5, 2017 classified 19 of them, to mention some :

DUCHENNE SMILE, FEAR SMILE, MISERABLE SMILE, DAMP SMILE, EMBARRASSED SMILE, CONTEMPT SMILE, THE MALICIOUS JOY and FAKE SMILE while Matthew Sweet identifies 16 types of smiles, some are similar with health and Fitness while others were added by him, in his list he included:

1. The Love Smile.

According to Sweet, this is the one reserved for someone you love. It's like a secret handshake. And when you're in it, nothing else matters. It is like 'you have killed me dear!'

2. The Old Friend Smile.

You're meeting someone you haven't seen for a long time. You embrace. You look at each other. Your smile says, "I missed you." Long time seen. It is like bringing back the old memories. Long time ago!

3. The Fake Smile.

We use this when we know we should smile, but don't feel like it. We think nobody can see it's insincerity, but we're fooling ourselves. People see our cheating though they do not tell us.

4. The Victory Smile.

You got the job or passed exams. You closed the deal. Some smiles are for life's little victories. It is like winning. This one is for the big wins and the landmarks. This is the one one claps inside hi or her heart.

5. The Surrender Smile.

It can get no worse. Everything has been taken from you. You are broken. You have nothing left. You have no more tears and no more screams left to expel. All you can do is smile at how ridiculous this thing called life can be.

6. The Malicious Smile.

Someone you hate has just failed. Your rival is collapsing and burning. When we take pleasure in the misfortunes and suffering of others. 'Aha,good! he got it'

7. The Lonely Smile.

The smile you have when no one is looking. When you are alone with your troubles, your fears, your worries, your anxiety. Or when you are thinking of the people around you and the richness of the world in your heart.

WHY DO PEOPLE SMILE?

According to Charles Darwin, as he was described in Oral health Foundation said that smiling is truly universal. A thing involving the whole world, all of us understand meaning of smiles and the feeling behind it. Darwin also distinguished smiling from laughter (although he admitted that both often appear at the same time). He believed laughter was connected to an amusement but the smile was grater sign of joy and happiness. Smile shows not only happiness, it also shows our emotion and joy to others. No need of telling anyone you are happiness, smile alone says a lot.

According to many scientific researches,our brains react to what our body is doing and it can have a knock on effect to our emotions. If we put smile, according to these findings, whether we are genuinely happy or not, our brains will interpret it as happiness and hence change our mood automatically. Here we may conclude by saying that, we add more happiness in every time we smile. According to this research, it takes 43 muscles to flown but only 17 to smile. So if one needs to save his/her efforts let him/her smile than sulking. Every time we are natural, we give a natural smile but if we are not we give an artificial smile or fake smile. Smile can be broad, sincere, dramatic or spontaneous. Smiles look different depending the muscles we use in our face lips, cheeks or eyes. They can be polite or warm, endearing or symmetrical, miserable or lopsided. The findings conclude by saying that people smile to express their inner personalities.

Openness, Conscientiousness, Extra version, Agreeableness and Neurotic-ism (People who respond worse to stress and are more likely to interpret ordinary situations as threatening and minor frustrations as hopelessly difficult, over exaggerators)

ARRIVING TO THE SMILING NATION.

As soon as the writer came out of his flight, he saw a security man smiling at him. 'sir' he said, " Your 'kababayan' is waiting for you there" What is kababayan? Does this person know me? But he is smiling at me! 'Well let me see', the author said to himself. Indeed, the one person whose appearance resembling the writer was outside. There he guessed that may be 'kababyan' meant 'someone from one's own country or village or who looks like him. That was in August 4, 2006 in Manila, Philippines.

STUDYING CEBUANO LANGUAGE IN DAVAO WITH SMILING TEACHERS.

One of the moments of joy and discovery was the time of learning a new culture and new language. This was a moment of fear of a new language but due to the smiling faces of Filipino teachers welcoming the writer, the fear left him and so he became more courageous than before. Smile removes unnecessary fear.

The first day the classroom: National Anthem and its meaning.

The teacher told the Author that they were going to learn both Tagalog and Cebuano (Bisaya) versions. That some days would be Tagalog while other days Cebuano Language. What does it mean? What is the origin? What is its English translation? The learning started anyway:

Bisaya Yutang Tabunon

Yutang tabunon
Mutya nga masilakon
Putling bahandi
Amo kang gimahal

Mithing gisimba
Yuta's mga bayani
Sa malupigon
Padagapigan ka

Ang mga bungtod mo ug lapyahan
Ang langit mong bughaw
Nagahulad sa awit, lamdag sa
Kaliwat tang gawas

Silaw sa adlaw ug bitoon
Sa nasudnong bandila
Nagatimaan nga buhion ta
Ang atong pagkausa

Yutang maanyag, duyan ka sa pagmahal,
Landong sa langit ang dughan mo;
Pakatam-ison namo kon maulipon ka
Ang kamatayon sa ngalan mo.

This first week made the writer to do some little history about the song in a small Library in the Language school. Aha, he realized that the song was composed by Julian Filipe and he found out that the song was in Spanish even though by that time the writer was learning it by heart both the Cebuano and Tagalog versions of Philippine National Anthem. He therefore, went and checked on the internet and printed all of them and placed them at the door of his room. Not only that but he also downloaded the notes of the music to be able to play on his Keyboard before he went to sleep daily for one month.

Julian Felipe

Original Spanish Version
Marcha Nacional Filipina (1899)

Tierra adorada
Hija del sol de Oriente,
Su fuego ardiente
En ti latiendo está.

¡Tierra de amores!
Del heroísmo cuna,
Los invasores
No te hollarán jamás.

En tu azul cielo, en tus auras,
En tus montes y en tu mar
Esplende y late el poema
De tu amada libertad.

Tu pabellón, que en las lides
La victoria iluminó,
No verá nunca apagados
Sus estrellas ni su sol.

Tierra de dichas, del sol y amores,
En tu regazo dulce es vivir.
Es una gloria para tus hijos,
Cuando te ofenden, por ti morir.

Official Commonwealth-Era
English Version
The Philippine Hymn (1938)
Land of the morning
Child of the sun returning
With fervor burning
Thee do our souls adore.

Land dear and holy,
Cradle of noble heroes,
Ne'er shall invaders
Trample thy sacred shores.

Ever within thy skies and through thy clouds
And o'er thy hills and sea
Do we behold the radiance, feel the throb
Of glorious liberty

Thy banner dear to all our hearts
Its sun and stars alight,
Oh, never shall its shining fields
Be dimmed by tyrants might!

Beautiful land of love, o land of light,
In thine embrace 'tis rapture to lie
But it is glory ever, when thou art wronged
For us, thy sons to suffer and die

Bayang Magiliw,
Perlas ng Silanganan
Alab ng puso
Sa Dibdib mo'y buhay.

Lupang Hinirang,
Duyan ka ng magiting,
Sa manlulupig
Di ka pasisiil

Sa dagat at bundok,
Sa simoy at sa langit mong bughaw,
May dilag ang tula
At awit sa paglayang minamahal.

Ang kislap ng watawat mo'y
Tagumpay na nagniningning;
Ang bituin at araw niya,
Kailan pa ma'y di magdidilim

Lupa ng araw, ng luwalhati't pagsinta,
Buhay ay langit sa piling mo;
Aming ligaya na pag may mang-aapi,
Ang mamatay nang dahil sa iyo.

Lupang Hinirang

JULIAN FELIPE

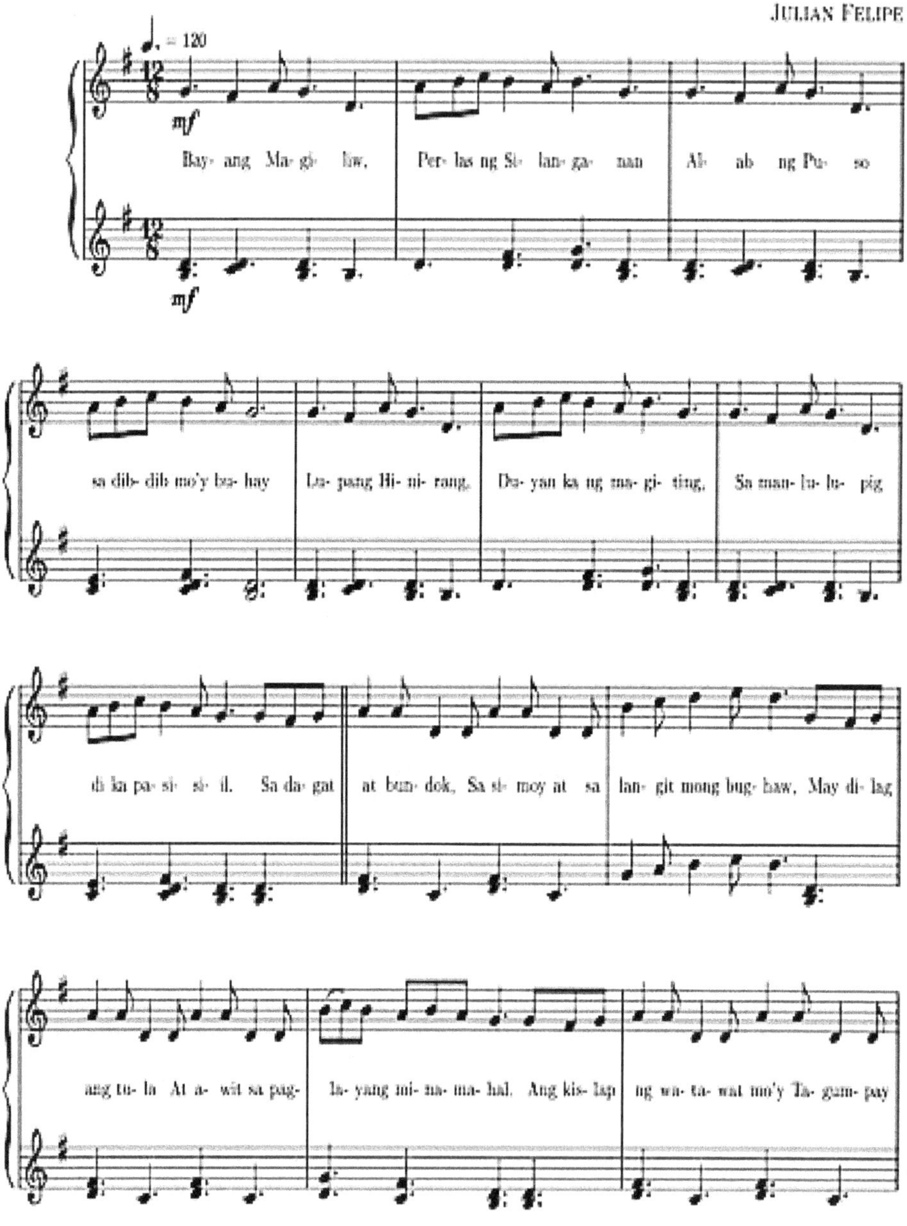

The Second week.

Learning Filipino Culture.

The beauty of the country is felt when one learns peoples' culture which is the totality of peoples' life (Language, food, walking, houses, customs, dressing etc). Learning Bisaya was not only sweet but also vocalic. Most of Filipino languages are so musical, they are spoken with a musical tone. That was the second week of joy. Questions using partical ba, Kinsa (man), who?Unsa (man) What?, Kanus-a (man) when? Unsang orasa (man) what time?. All these broght an eye open to the writer. Then the 'music' went on, this time 'Diin', Hain or Asa (man) Where then Past,present and future time were introduced. The first Musical sentence was: **Tapulan ba si Nonoy? Is Nonoy lazy**? In mornings the teachers taught grammar but in the evening was time of stories, practice and fun, time for more expressions. This time the first expression was about greeting and getting acquainted Formally: Kumusta ka? How are you? The fun thing in this was that, every one including the sick in the hospitals replied 'Ok rang'...may be with some addition later with Maarang-arang na (it is improving), sometimes it was at a critical moment. Have you seen someone dying telling you he/she is ok?

That took the learners to the third week where they continued to learn about positive common expressions like 'A GOOD PERSON', maayoong ang tawo, KIND, buotan, CAN BE TRUSTED, kasaligan, NOT STURBBON, humuk ug ulo, RELIGOUS, hinimbahon,UNDERSTANDING, masinabtanon, MERCIFUL, maluloy-on and HOSPITABLE, Maabiabihon. The list continued day after another. Apart from these, there was a tip in making life better. Since Filipino language borrowed some words from Spanish language, one could use Spanish words and make a sense. Words like Gwapa, Gwapo (beautiful, handsome) in case one forgot a name. Even counting in Spanish also could bring meaning to the people. When it came to counting one to twenty, they were taught both, Cebuano counting and Spanish counting. Both are clear in the market, the Spanish one was easily because it resembles to many European languages that one learns in his or her life:

Uno ....one
Dos..two
Tres.. three
cuatro..four
cinco..five
seis...six
siete...seven
ocho..eight
nueve..nine
diez..ten

once..eleven

doce..twelve

trece..thirteen

catorce..fourteen

quince..fifteen

dieciseis..sixteen

diecisiete..seventeen

dieciocho..eighteen

diecinueve..nineteen

Veinte/Bayte..twenty

RIDDLES.

The Fouth week: Riddles (Tigmo) This is a question or statement intending to require ingenuity in ascertaining its answer or meaning. This was not only learning a language but it involved thinking, trying to figure out as what exactly needed. There are few which children could guess easily.

1. DUNA KOY HIGALA, BISAN ASA KUYOG GYUD SIYA, SA TUBIG DI MALUMOS,SA KALAYO DI MASUNOG (I have a friend, anywhere I go he goes with me, in the water, he won't drown, in fire, he won't burn). The Answer here is ANINO (Shadow). Wherever we go, we move with our shadow. This riddle makes us to think more, we may think also about our being, our 'mes' our 'Is', our human experience, our relation with others, our cultures and values,understanding, helping others etc.

2. TAAS KUN MALINKOD, MUBO KUN MAGTINGDOG. (Tall when sitting, short when standing). IRO (A dog). This riddle teaches us another lesson in a human experience. It is not always getting alright when we achieve more, sometimes success happen in our lives when we are not promoted, learned, employed. On the other hand some people fail when they are employed, promoted or well educated.

3. USA KA DALAGA MAY KORONA, BISAN ASA DUNAY MATA. (One maiden with a crown, with eyes all over). PINYA (Pineapple). In a human experience this riddle goes beyond a pineapple, it reflects about different persons with different visions in life. They see many things at one time. These are people who may think where they came from, where they are going to, what is found on the left, right, north, south, east and west. People of many-vision. People of many eyes can have good future. Having many eyes is having a sense of 'looking around oneself' where are you from? What are you doing? Why are you doing what you are doing? Isn't it a smile here?

4. SA ILALUM KABATOAN SA IBABAW KAGANGSANGAN. (Underneath it is rocky, on top it is very rough). DURIAN (Durian). This beautiful fruit which is popular in Davao shows two dimensions of a human life: goodness and badness. Many people do not like the smell of Durian. After eating it, go across a street, people will know that you have eaten Durian. Despite this feared smell, Durian is so delicious. You hear Davao children remarking, LAMI, (delicious).

To experience this flavor of Durian, one needs to be courageous to climb the tree, to hold the Durian fruits which are surrounded by thrones, to open the inside and eventually find the flesh of it. All these require efforts, patience, courage and resilience. This riddle teaches us that life consists of suffering, suffering is in us, we need to toil in order to achieves our goals.

IDIOMATIC EXPRESSIONS.

The Fifth week. Idiomatic Expression. These are sayings that are commonly used but their meanings can not be determined by the individual words in the saying itself. This was another week of sharpening students' brains. One needed to think and think for him or her to get a correct answer. It took almost three weeks to get used to the expressions but all of them were one of the sources of joy and smile.

1. Klaro sama sa lapok, (As clear as mud, lit) meaning - Not clear. As students were moving from one street to another, sometimes the old people used this expression, "Aha, Maayo kaayo kay kabalo ka bisaya, apan ang imong bisaya morag klaro sama sa lapok (So, you know Cebuano language,that is very good even though your Cebuano is as clear as mud) meaning they did not understand what these students were try to talk.

The Sixth week: In this week the learners were introduced to physical feelings:

Gimingaw ako...I am lonely.

Gibati ako ug paghiguguma...................I feel I am in love.

Gikapoy ako...I am tired.

Gilaay ako...I am bored.

Gimingaw ako nimu.................................I miss you.

Gitugnaw siya...He felt cold.

Girayuma siya...He has arthritis.

Giregla siya...She has menstruation.

Gihubagan siya.......................................He has a boil.

Gisingot siya...He is sweating.

Gisip-on ko...I have cold.

The list continued till the seventh week when the learner entered into story telling in Cebuano. In this part Dialogues were introduced to the learners. This was a very important part of life with people. It was so because they were trained to live with people in different places of the country.

The first dialogue was greetings PANGUMUSTA.

In this first dialog the writer was acting as an old man (Tigulan) while one of his classmate acted as a single lady (Dalaga)

Tigulan: Asa ka man Day, sayo pa man? (Young woman, too early, where are you going to?)

Dalaga: Diha lang Noy. (Just there, Grand pa)

Tigulan: Kumusta na ang imong Tatay? (How is you dady)

Dalaga: Maayo man kalooy sa Diyos. Sige Noy, adto na ko (By the grace of God, he is doing fine, sorry Grand, i need to go)

Tigulang: Sige Day (Alright)

There the lady left an old man in peace. The old man was not aware of the mood of the girl but all he knew was a smile from the girl and that life moves on.

Polite refusal is very common, sometimes one hears, 'we shall see next time' once this word is spoken, most probably the answer is no! For foreigners, it can be a moment of waiting and waiting until the giving up moment arrives while for Filipino themselves message sent, there was a refusal. Now you know that it is very rare to hear a word no from the mouth of a polite Filipino.

It is such a polite way which makes Philippines so unique. Very rare will you find people in office addressing your name directly. They instead address you by introducing, Sir or Mam even when you have done something wrong eg 'Sir. It is not allowed to park here, you will pay 500 pesos' Isn't it a good thing?

Apart from the first dialogue, the writer learned other expressions:

Maayong buntag-Good morning

Duagay ka man lagi-You are late

Gipakyaw man nimo ang tindahan- It seems you bought the whole store

Ginhawa pa- Still breathing.

Buhi pa gihapon-Still alive

Gwapo (pogi) lang gihapon-Still handsome

Ulitawo pa intawon-Still a bachelor, pity

Tiawtiaw ka baya-You are joking

Pag-ayo-ayo, ha?-Good luck. Do well.

EXPRESSIONS

One of the sweetest parts of any Filipino language is an expression. Most of these expressions carry the whole entire culture of the community. Sometime one hears someone saying 'Hoy Salamat sa Dios abot na' (thanks be to God I have arrived). This indicates the person's culture is the culture which puts God first in all things.

The second part of the dialogue was introducing oneself and introducing others, **PAGPA-ILA-ILA.** In this part of Dialogue there were two persons acting as Ben (B) and Lina (L) and Alice (Alice).

B. Uy, Lina, kinsa man nag kauban nimo? (Lina, who is with you?)

L. Ai, Ben, kini si Alice ang akong higala (My friend Alice)

B. Kumusta. (How (Are you?)

A. Maayo man. Silingan diay mo ni Lina? (Ok, so, I see you are neighbors)

B. Oo. Ikaw hain man dapit ang inyong balay? (Yes we are, and you, where are you from?)

A. Taga-Cebu gyud ko. Miduaw ko dinhi. (I am from Cebu, I came to visit)

B. Paisano diay ta. (we are all town mate)

L.Sigi Ben, mouna mi nimo (Ok, Ben, we are going ahead of you)

In this Dialogue the writer learned that, usually many people do not be alone, do not walk alone. In a normal circumstance one needs a friend to be with. Wherever the youth will be parents must ask who is with him or her.

The sixth week. Real life in the Philippines began.

On this week Culture was on of the areas that the author of this lived experience focused. It was this time when he was able to say his first mass in Cebuano Language. The first day was filled with mistakes in pronunciation. It was difficult due to the changes in this language where by a word beginning with 'Ju' can be sometimes pronounced 'Ju' or 'hu' let say the gospel according to John is pronounced HUAN. One thing which was so interesting was a smile. Sometimes one could give a correction on the spot but the rest could be looking at the author and smiled.

STREET, MARKET, JEEPNEY AND MALLS EXPERIENCE.

Filipinos avoid shame (ulaw) and so if one is doing something without shame will be looked at as a person without discipline.

Sometimes when one can be praised for a nice dress the response could be simple.

Try to follow the talk of two women the author found at the Mall.

Woman 1- Uy, nindot ang imong sinina! (hala, your dress is so beautiful)

Woman 2-Sinana lang ba diay, unsay man ang nawong nako? (So, is it only my dress, what about my face?)

Woman 1-Gwapa pud apan ang sinina nimo morag ang Angel. (Also beautiful but the dress looks like of an angel).

Woman 2-(Smiling) Barato uy! ukay ukay ani. (it is so cheap from the second hand market)....all smiling.Traveling with Jeep is another fun life one can experience in the country. Most of the Jeeps in the evening are full but with little complain.Most of the Jeeps in the evening are full but with little complain. Most of the time one hears 'excuse me, Ser, Maam excuse me, munaug nako' (Kindly maam/sir give way I am dropping).The biggest wonder is the Jeepney's driver. Most of them do not have conductors. The driver does almost 7 jobs alone: Driving, collecting money, stopping almost everywhere when some one calls dri lang! (here please), giving back change, calling for passengers to come in, announcing the stations ahead of him, tuning the sound system of his radio, looking on the side mirror who did not pay and remind him or her while smiling, looking at the side morrow so that he does not knock another car etc. When one looks at a Jeepney Filipino drivers smiles too. These are model of hard working class in the world, it is amazing! Mabuhay Filipino Jeepney driviers!

Pass on the street, notice poor families but look at them, you will meet a smiling face. One may keep on asking "do they know me?"In this dialogue what came into the mind of the writer was that the Filipino refuse to say or tell in a polite way. It is difficult to hear I SAY NO! but 'we shall see, next time, let us wait and see, ugma na lang (tomorrow). In the dialogue above, the young lady did not want her grandpa to know exact place where she was heading to and she said 'Diha lang' (somewhere unknown), and when she was tired of her grand pa questions, instead of saying 'excuse me am not ready to answer your many questions for i have many other business, she simply begins by saying 'sege Noy' (Alright Grand Pa, I appreciate, let me go).Try to go to the market and hear the talk among the buyers and sellers. Most of them strive so hard especially in Markets which are not well constructed. You meet them sweating, no electric fun, sometimes it rains on them but they can not miss a smile even when they are crossing a drainage system.

Other things that brought joy on this week was to meet the things that the author learned at school about Filipino culture, to mention some: HARANA (to serenade, courting a young lady, 'dalaga', sometimes the man went with a guitar to the house of a girl singing a love song), PAG AMIN (the kissing of hand of to the forehead as a sign of respect to the elders), PAMISTA (A celebration of a patron saint of a certain church or chapel), BUYAG/ PUYRA BUYAG (is uttered when a compliment is given to a person, this is to let disease get away from him/her, it is superstition anyway).

WHY DO FILIPINO SMILE?

This may not be a simple question but based on Filipino themselves we can try to answer.Most people say that only those people having plenty of money and wealth experience happiness, but this is not the case here. This country disapprove this statement. Most of the Filipino are not material rich but Spiritually rich. The love of God, hope, religion inside their lives and some other reasons all make them hope for tomorrow. Do not try to remove smile among the Filipinos by wishing them a natural calamity like typhoon, earthquake and many others you will never remove a smile on their faces. Let be hunger, imprisonment, death, war or poverty, always smile will be there. They will tell you BAHALA NA (come what may).

This community is fixed in hope. Each person says 'There is goodness still to come, life has to move on, let problems be there but I must sleep, I am counting my blessings not the ones I am missing, since I am still alive God has given me a chance to move on, I should not worry so much'. Philippines is a country filled with brave people. If it is a mark of resilience that God gave to humanity, then Filipino got it clearly.

WHERE DO FILIPINO LEARN THIS BEAUTIFUL VALUE OF RESILIENCE?

The very simple answer could be parents. Parents are playing a great role to sharpening their children at home. However we based on Filipino history, it is good to look around the global. T

The idea that life consists of suffering is within the community. One may also think of the influence of world Philosophers especially the biggest Philosophers. Let us speculate and see around the world where this spirit may relate with.

THE DIFFERENCES AND SIMILARITIES BETWEEN WORLD PHILOSOPHY WITH FILIPINO PHILOSOPHY.

a) AFRICAN PHILOSOPHY- <u>UBUNTU.</u> This is a Nguni bantu term that refers to "humanity". In other words it talks about humanity towards others. It is the belief in the universality that connects all human beings. This mostly applied in many black African communities: 'I am because you are, and because you are, therefore I am'. This means, life becomes meaningful if one relates well with others. According to this Philosophy, selfishness is an enemy of humanity with development.

b) WESTERN PHILOSOPHY.

<u>SOCRATES:</u> According to this first giant thinker, a person must discover his life's purpose, discover who he is, mission and what he is trying to become.

Kosages in his writings tried to expand what it means to be to your true self: Be who you want to be and create unusual things to unlock your true potential, live a happier life, make other people happier and make our planet a greater place. Also Kosages adds, small dreams, small breakthroughs, big dreams, big breakthroughs. He asks why then to walk if you can fly?. Therefore, dare to live, dream big dreams, live as you believe and do not sit on your dreams. He adds more that one does not need to watch news but to create news.In order to do this one must make a strategic decision.

While tying to be a better person, one should not try to be better than everyone else but rather becoming better than the previous day knowing that average ones compete with others while great ones compete with themselves. He concludes by saying challenges bring about excitement. So stretch yourself. If you live what you do, there is no difficult task, only intensifying ones. Hence, pursue your dreams, there is a sea of treasures just under your feet.   Back to Socrates, we may summarize his work as it was well portrayed by THE SCHOOLOF LIFE. Namely: One. **Care for your soul**. Two. **Knowledge is necessary to become virtuous and virtue is necessary to attain happiness**. Three. **All evil acts are committed out of ignorance and hence involuntarily**. Four. **Committing an injustice is far worse than suffering an injustice**.

Here Socrates calls all human to do what is just to each other, killing someone for example does not create happiness to the killer but it brings more pain to the killer in his/her life entirely. In the Philippines Parents pass values to their children that apart from undergoing through difficult life, they should not give up but believe in god. This is a very important knowledge in a human person life.

PLATO: Plato insisted that a human person needs to find fulfillment in his life which he called *Eudaimonia*. The main ideas that Plato brings about are: One.**Think more**. In whatever things we do in life, we need to think. Plato insists on knowing oneself and avoiding hear say what he calls **Doxa**. Two. **Let your lover change you**. There is a need to improve in a human life day after another until he/she becomes a better person for true love is admiration. He insists that a couple should not love each other exactly as they are right now. There must be a change to betterment from previous years to the following years always. Three. **Decode the message of beauty.** In order to bring beauty one needs to renounce selfishness, learn to be generous and to be modest, these would result into: *Gentleness, Harmony, Balance, Peace and Strength*.

Four. **Reform the society**. According to Plato, the society needs to produce fulfilling persons.When the time of vote comes people need to think properly why they vote, they should not vote until they start thinking rationally that is to say until they become philosophers. On the other side politicians should become philosophers that is to say Kings become philosophers or philosophers Kings. If we look what brings the beauty to the Filipino people is not the material things they have but, smile, resilience, harmony and the strength they have. Peace is disrupted sometimes in some parts of the country but every time they fall they get up immediately and walk.

ARISTOTLE: Aristotle's can be summarized when looking at the main questions he asked: **a) What makes people happy?** After doing his intellectual findings, Aristotle thought that happiness is been achieved not by having plenty of well to do or material possessions but rather happiness is achieved by having *virtue*. Aristotle identified eleven virtues: *Courage, Temperance, Liberality, Magnificence, Magnanimity, Pride, Patience, Truthfulness, Witness, Friendliness and Modest*. According to him in every virtue a person needs a golden mean. The desirable middle between two extremes, one of excess and the other of deficiency example Courage is between the two; Cowardice- COURAGE-Rashness. Also, Shamelesness-MODESTY-Shyness.Unambitiousness-PRIDE-Ambition. Lack of spirit-PATIENCE-Irascibility. Underestatement-TRUTHFULNESS-Boastfulness. **b) What art for?** In this Aristotle discusses about peripeteia (change of fortune), Anagnoresis (dramatic revelation) and Catharsis (cleaning up our emotions). In other words we need arts to change our lives to betterment. **c) What are friends for?** Aristotle explains three kinds of friends: For fun, Aquitances and a true friend. People move together to enjoy, some work together simply because they belong to one company or sport team but a true friend is he/she who loves you no matter what you are or have. In short is a selfless person to you. d) How can ideas cut through in a busy world? People are busy but that does not make them not to understand things. Aristotle talks about Rhetoric (the art of getting people to agree with you).

ORIENTAL PHILOSOPHY.

When we talk about oriental we speak about East. This therefore, include the Philippines. In this case the the group consist of Philosophers from Eastern side of the world. There Philosophers are many but to mention some:
Buddha, Confucius and Lao Tzu.

BUDDHA.

Looking at Buddha's Philosophy one may connect well with the filipino resilience and survival life. Let us look at the main teachings he gave:

The three universal truths.

i.Nothing is lost in the universe.

In this first universal truth Buddha says that

Matter turns into energy, energy turns into matter. It is like a recycle in our modern language. A dead leaf turns into soil. A seed sprouts and becomes a new plant. Old solar systems disintegrate and turn into cosmic rays. We are born of our parents, our children are born of us and life continues like that.

While looking at plants, trees and ourselves as humans, we realize that we are the same. We consist of that which is around us, we are the same as everything. If we destroy something around us, we destroy ourselves. If we cheat another, we cheat ourselves, if we kill others, we kill ourselves. If we hate others we hate ourselves. Understanding this truth, the Buddha and his disciples never killed any animal. The last point is not matching well with the Filipino culture where animals especially pigs are killed daily for Lechon (Roasted meat). However the belief of the continuity of life even when we die is almost similar.

ii. Everything changes

In this Buddha said that life is like a river flowing on and on, ever-changing. The earth changes, the concepts changes. Our ideas about life also change. People once believed that the world was flat, but now we know that it is round.

iii.Law of cause and effect.

In this Buddha speaks about **KARMA**, this is a destiny following as effect from cause. In this third concept Buddha said that nothing ever happens to us unless we deserves it. We receive exactly what we earn, whether it is good or bad. In this we are called to think in whatever we do for that is what we shall experience. What We are, the way we are now is due to the things we have done in the past. Our thoughts and actions determine the kind of life we can have. If we do good things, in the future good things will happen to us. If we do bad things, in the future bad things will happen to us. Every moment we create new karma by what we say, do, and think. Buddha said,

"The kind of seed sown
will produce that kind of fruit.
Those who do good will reap good results.
Those who do evil will reap evil results.
If you carefully plant a good seed,
You will joyfully gather good fruit." Is this concept present among the Filipinos? Yes, most of the Filipino believe in God and that what we do to others here on earth will definitely be rewarded by God when we meet Him.

THE FOUR NOBLE TRUTHS

1. Life consists of suffering. There sufferings are like: birth, sickness, death, old age, being with those we dislike, stay far from those we love, not getting what we want, failure in our goals, disappointments, when we are betrayed by those who loved us etc. Buddha does not deny happiness but he insists that apart from the happy life we may experience, indeed we can not escape from suffering. Suffering is therefore real.
2. There is cause of Suffering. Buddha identify two things as cause of suffering as ignorance and greed.. The things people want most cause them the most suffering. I want, I want, I want,

I want...well, there are basic things that all people should have and not greed, like adequate food, shelter, and clothing. Everyone deserve a good home, loving parents, and good friends. They should enjoy life and cherish their possessions without becoming greedy.

3. Suffering has an end. According to Buddha when we end greed and embrace a natural way and peaceful way there we end suffering. That is to experience *Nirvana*. which is an everlasting state of peace, happiness and joy. 4. We can end suffering if we follow the Path. These are the eight fold:

1. **Right View**. The right way to think about life is to see the world through the eyes of the Buddha--with wisdom and compassion.

2. **Right Thought**. We are what we think. Clear and kind thoughts build good, strong characters, bad thought build bad character.

3. **Right Speech**. There is a need to have a bank of words. By speaking kind and helpful words, we are respected and trusted by everyone.

4. **Right Conduct**. These are actions we do. No matter what we say, others know us from the way we behave. Before we criticize others, we should first see what we do ourselves.

5. **Right Livelihood**. Not everyone who is rich earned it using the right way. Some got it after exploiting others. Buddha insist on choosing a job that does not hurt others. The Buddha said, "Do not earn your living by harming others. Do not seek happiness by making others unhappy."

6. **Right Effort**. A worthwhile life means doing our best at all times and having good will toward others. This also means not wasting effort on things that harm ourselves and others.

7. **Right Mindfulness**. This means being aware of our thoughts, words, and deeds. What goes on inside your minds does a lot to make you as you.

8. **Right Concentration**. Focus on one thought or object at a time. By doing this, we can be quiet and attain true peace of mind.

LAO TZU

TAO TE CHING

Knowing others is wisdom;

Knowing the self is enlightenment.

Mastering others requires force;

Mastering the self requires strength;

He who knows he has enough is rich.

Perseverance is a sign of will power.

He who stays where he is endures.

To die but not to perish is to be eternally present.

Nb: Can we say also the Filipinos got something from these Philosophers?

CONFUCIUS.

His social philosophy was based primarily on the principle of "ren" or "loving others" while exercising self-discipline. He believed that ren could be put into action using the Golden Rule, "What you do not wish for yourself, do not do to others." (Lunyu 12.2, 6.30).

FILIPINO PHILOSOPHY AND VALUES AS MAIN SOURCES OF THEIR SMILE.

According to free Dictionary, value is a principle or stand, as of behavior, that is considered important or desirable. The Summary of Filipino values can be found into three Tagalog words:

SILA (They,them), TAYO (We,ours), AKO (Me, mine).

The Filipinos thinks about others first, then look at the 'we', 'our' before they think of themselves 'ako' it is such a selfless life towards others.

Soul lifters of the weak, the wounded and the forgotten communities.

Philippines like many other nations in the world experience so many challenges. Most of these challenges are natural and some are man made.

These natural challenges include: Typhoon, flood, heavy rain and volcano. Man made challenges include: Poverty, war, Political parties and high population. Despite all these challenges they suffer, Filipinos can lift one another to create hope, peace and SMILE. Whenever you hear any of these happening, go and for sure you will find someone there is helping already. These people helping others are not only the rich but also the poor and the lonely. Filipinos do not become silent when others are suffering.

During Typhoon 'wash' 'Sendong' for example, there were so many groups who went to rescue Iligan City survivors. They constructed new houses, classrooms, toiletries and provided social service to them. Others were looking for help from all over to help their fellow Filipinos in trouble. These includes our Late Rt Bishop Galido DD (The Bishop of Iligan by then), Jonny and Bingle (Left below) who not only helped during time of suffering to build shelters, classroom, Madrassah and Mosques but he is still lifting up his fellow men and women through Adult Literacy till now. Such a good man!

Above: One of the 5 Mosques and a Muslim village built by the Church and Bingle's efforts.

You come and see people who lost their family member two days ago, smiling, they do so due to many factors but one of them are people who hold them their shoulders like Bingle. In life while crying, if you find a friend beside you, you will get hope to move on, to walk and to wake up the next morning. The government also is sometimes listens to the people and helps them to move on. The Department of education in Iligan District was not left behind to help those who were affected by typhoon to ensure that education continues to reach the unreachable and the less privileged communities. Below: ALS (Alternative Learning System from Iligan in Action).

Caring for elders.

Filipino do not think of sending their old ones to the elderly homes but they think of staying with them no matter what. We do not deny that there are homes for the elderly nowadays but what we want here to say is that majority of the Filipinos are not comfortable to sending their elders to those homes. The Filipinos take care of their elders by taking them into their homes.

Politeness

People address you using Sir/mam. They are people who respect others. Very rare do they call baptismal names, most of the times they address nicknames with Sir/mam, and at the end Thank you so much, Salamat Po! Or upo.
Wherever one goes being in the schools or business, one finds a smile with a welcome. 'welcome sir!' 'welcome mam' At time people buy commodities not because they like the commodities sold but because of the welcome they receive.

Gratitude

Gratitude or '"utang na loob" or "Utang sa kabubut on" If at all you have done something good to a person, wait to hear from him or her a dept of gratitude. Filipinos do not forget the goodness done to them. It is very common to hear mass for thanksgiving for the blessings received from God. Mass for one year of Kios business, Mass to thank God for passing board exam, birthday anniversary of their grand pa who died in 1803. If one comes a different culture will wait to see if the birthday celebrant is around only later one will realize that in fact the birthday celebrant is no more. All these is to show that they are today because of somebody's life who lived before them. Helping a Filipino is like a bank deposit, they may not necessarily pay you materially but for sure they will pray for you.

Hospitality

Hospitality is everywhere in the Philippines. The Filipinos are very hospitable when it comes to their fellowmen. They will invite their visitors to come into their homes and offer them treats such as snacks and drinks after a long journey. Some especially in village areas they will go the extremes as to give up the comfort of their own bedrooms for their guests and to the point of sleeping on floor just to ensure that their guests are comfortable.They do not mind to suffer for some nights just to let the new comer enjoy their comfort zone. This culture is so common in many African societies. One can wonder, where do Filipino get this beautiful attitude.

Lovers of Saints and procession.

The Philippines is one among the biggest countries where saints are respected more and their life is celebrated by the entire community.

Where there is a Catholic Chapel or Church , there one finds a Patron saint and eventually the feast day of a chapel (PIESTA/FIESTA).

There are some devotions which can be found only in the Philippines like Santo Niño and Black Nazarene. Santo Niño refers to the Holy Child (Jesus).c According to Thomas M. Landy, this is an image of a small boy typically dressed like a King. Devotion to Him are part of every parish in the Philippines. One can find this image in almost every Catholic home. Some Filipinos working abroad carry it too. Cebu can be called as the central part of the entire celebration. To trace back the History of Santo Niño one need got mentions the Spanish colonial time. Come on the second week of January to Cebu and see the joyful faces of the Filipinos! Filipinos travel from all over the country to join the celebration.

See the street dancers without shoes dancing early in the morning! One may wonder, where are these people getting this joy? Sometimes the events draws up to 1.5 million participants (Thomas M. Landy). Those who can not make it to Cebu usually celebrate at home (see the book cover of this book). Below: Santo Niño

Another Celebration is so unique, the Black Nazarene (Poong na Nazareno see the above). This is a life-sized black statue of a suffering Jesus fallen under the weight of the cross. It is almost 7 km route from Luneta where the Park is to the Basilica of Quiapo. This is another unique celebration in the Philippines which brings together almost 2million people together. Usually the number of devotees surrounding the procession (See the above).

To understand this event one needs to go back to 1787 when Tanslacion (transfer) took place from its original home where Rizal park is now located to its present home which is now known as Quiapo. Many Filipino consider it as a miraculous statue that as they attend the procession, they receive, healing from terminal cancers and other sickness, to grant petitions, and to help those in need and the suffering. Come also to join this celebration (but if you are strong). Pushing, scrambling for towels which touched the original image takes place here. For an outsider like me this procession is dangerous but see the faces of the Filipinos on procession, they have no giving up heart. (we must finish, they say).

Family

The Philippines value their families. The Filipinos recognize their family as an important social structure that one must take care of. It is the first thing to thing about as a Filipino. They give importance to the safety and unity of one's family. This intact is so common among the Filipino family that it is common for members of the same family work for the same company so long as they are together.

Family here does not mean Father, mother and child but it extends to grands, uncles, unties pets etc. It is also common to find the whole clan living in the same area. Filipinos are afraid to be too far from their own family, but many are far in the whole world? The answer is, **SACRIFICE**. Sometimes in some occasions all the family members share one room on the floor with smiles without any complain. It is amazing!

Loyalty

Loyalty or '''Pakikisama''' is another Filipino value. Filipinos are loyal to their friends and people, they ensure the peace in the group. They have a sense of justice and fairness and concern for others with their well being. Filipinos recognize the essential humanity of all people and regard others with respect and empathy. With this orientation, Filipinos develop a sensitivity to the nature and quality of interpersonal relationships, which are their principal source of security and happiness".

Shame (ulaw, Hiya)

It is said that Filipinos would go to great lengths in order for one not to be ashamed. He /she without shame is regarded as a valueless person. As it was said before, it is better to miss something like food than been seen as a person without shame.

Creativity.

God created the world but Filipinos recreate the created things. Give them a chance to decorate, let them cook, let them do make ups to those going for a wedding. Give them a chance to design a dress for pageants, house etc. You will not regret for your choice.

Others are

Flexibility, Adaptability.

Filipino's sense of joy and humor is evident in their optimistic approach to life and its travails. The ability to laugh at themselves and their predicament is an important coping mechanism that contributes to emotional balance and a capacity to survive. These are manifested in the ability to adjust to often difficult circumstances and prevailing physical and social environments. Filipinos have a high tolerance for ambiguity that enables them to respond calmly to uncertainty or lack of information. Filipinos often improvise and make productive and innovative use of whatever is available. These qualities have been repeatedly demonstrated in their capacity to adapt to living in any part of the world and in their ability to accept change.

Hard work and Industrious people.

Filipinos are universally regarded as excellent workers who perform well whether the job involves physical labor and tasks or highly sophisticated technical functions. Above all, the Filipinos work with aim. They aim at something but mostly for their families. They may work anywhere in the world, leaving their beloved ones at home but knowing that freedom is coming tomorrow, A big smile is approaching, the next day is better than today. In the whole entire life of the researcher, he worked with different groups of Filipino but especially the marginalized groups. These were people who did not have a chance to go to school but today the story has changed after initiating **WE ARE MAD** (WE ARE MAKING A DIFFERENCE) program which was aiming at improving their standard of living. WHY? Because the Filipinos can change their miserable smile to an economical smile due to their hard work they endure and open to learn within a short period of time. The research was done in six barangays (sub districts) for six years and found that Filipino can change and improve their standard of life very fast. The next edition will give the finding of this economic smile the writer found from 2009 to 2014 in Barangay **Digkilaan, Mainit, Kalilanganan, Panarogangan, Dulag, and Rogongon. (see schooling for a purpose-Adam Bago Cssp).**

HOPE FOR THE FUTURE.

1) Mindanao, Iligan and Marawi will rise. Conflicts and wars sometimes make a community to loose hope. Do not be one of those loosing hope. Conflicts bear negatives but always positive things will come. We do not know when but whatever number of years, there will be a time when the paradise will come again. If the people of the forgotten mountains have seen a big smile, what about those in the cities?

2) Reduction of poverty is coming. A good number young people are schooling now. Most of them have gadgets,some are connected to Internets, they dream bigger and aim higher. This shows that the future for the youth is so brighter than now.

3) Any Filipino reading these prophetic message, smile but know that you are one of those who make the Philippines great again by starting yourself, then to your family, friends etc...

LAUGHTER :CHILDREN AND YOUNG PEOPLE'S QUESTIONS THAT YOU SHOULD NOT GET ANNOYED.

In many elementary and high schools children and youth are so friendly. They want to know, they are not worried so much of so many things, but they are open to ask visitors even fun questions. To a black man from Africa kindly do not get annoyed but try to instruct them the truth should you have time. In class you may show them pictures also if you have. The following are few questions a visitor may encounter with:

1. 'Hey, your country Africa, do you have rice like in the Philippines?

Answer. Africa in not a country, it is the second biggest continent in the world with 54 countries. Some of these countries are big producers of rice.

2. ' We have heard that Africa is a very poor continent, children no food, is it true?

Answer. No and Yes, Africa is a very rich continent, it has almost everything, every mineral but what you see on TV is not all the continent. Most of the poverty is because of scramble for natural resource. In fact, most of the worldly fastest economies are Africans, the gadgets we use, the cars we drive, the instruments in Laboratories, necklaces etc.., most of the minerals are from Africa. However , when it comes to capital income the answer is Yes but population wise Asia has more poor people than Africa..

3. 'All white men are rich people?'

Answer. No, not every white man is rich, they are white men

without good of life.

4. 'All white men are from America and they speak English'

Answer. No, not all white men speak English, and not all white

men are Americans. English is not a national language in USA,

it is an official language as it is in the Philippines.

5. 'The most beautiful people are only the whites, I hate

to be a Filipino, I wish I could change my skin with chemicals

and operate my nose to look smaller and long' (some espl.

girls) *Answer. All people are image of God, 'Imago Dei' and so*

there is no human person who is angrier before God, accept it,

you are beautiful, many countries also wish they could look like

Filipino. Do not bother so much on your color but on your

character and heart...what to focus mostly are :

Love, faith, respect, accepting to live together with any person,

harmony, unity,hope and above all your smile from your heart.

All these make one beautiful.

6. ' How come you are working on the mountainous areas,

those places are very far?'

Answer. A place is far if you do not like it or if you have no one

to care. If your ma'am is living on the mountain, you could be

visiting her every weekend because love conquers all including

the mountains.

Philippines Literature.

One of the areas that we may combine the totality of Filipino culture is   literature. One book written by   Bienvenido Lumbera gives the whole story of why Filipinos smile. For example when we read in his work we find Oral form (**1564)** like: Riddles, Proverbs, Short Poems, Ambahan and songs. Try to think a big house surrounded by many windows! What is the answer? <u>NET</u>. Next think of this proverb. 'Full of good cheer while borrowing a measure of rice, Full of wrath when you ask him to pay back'
Other works includes:

Lamge, Dangdang-Ay, An Balud, Pamuwa sa Bata, Muyin para Nino, Dumheb Ako a Dumanis. In Myth there is The Second Creation, The Great Flood and Tungkung Langit and Alunsina and others while folk tales includes The Story of the Orphan Girl, The Monkey and the Turtle. Some of the titles make one smile like a legend:How the Angels Built Lake Lanao. (Wo, so lake Lanao was built by Angels!)Here the knowledge of separation between Sebangan (East) and Sedpan (West) is explained. There is another aspect explained, epic: Tuwaang Attend a Wedding and Tuwaang in Battle. After reading this oral work where smiles can be originated there comes a written work during colonialism that is between **1565-1897 like**

Though it is Stormy and Dark The Children of Toil Must Now Be Heard and many others. Rizal with many great works which almost every Filipino is admiring are also contributing a lot to the country's smile.

Then came Emilio Jacinto who wrote 2 essays, Light and Darkness and the last mentioned by Bienvenido Lumbera was victoria Laktaw who wrote a poem 'Our Plea. All these literature work played a great role to the happy nation, The Philippines.

RELIGION IS LIFE

If there is a place where modernization failed to kill people's basic values is Philippines. God is still alive in the life of the

Filipinos. Richer or poorer, rain or shine God reigns and gives smile to his people. Nothing will separate them from God. If it is marriage could be a marriage beyond death. It is from this where the main source of smile is coming from. Let us see some Quotes from the Holy Bible where time of disasters some Filipino families read:

1. "Come to me, all you who are weary and burdened, and I will give you rest.

Take my yoke upon you and learn from me, for I am gentle and humble in heart, and you will find rest for your souls." Matthew 11:28-29

Actually there is a famous song for this known as Lift up your Hands composed by Cecile Azarcon. Speaking on a you tube Cecile encourages any one singing her song not to impress but to express. To thank God and acknowledge His presence among His people.

verse:C   Fm   C   Bb C7
Life is not that all that bad my friend, hmmm
 Fm7   G7   Em7
if you believe in your self, if you believe ther's someone who walks
             A
through life with you,
             Dm7   G7

you'll never be alone just learn to reach out

     Em7 A7

and open your heart,

  Dm7   G7sus4   G7   C

lift up your hands to God and hell show you the way

Chorus:C7   Fm7   G7sus4 G7   Em7

A7

And he said, "cast your burden up on me, those who are

havily laden,

     Dm7   Dm/C   G7

Come to me all of you who are lived of

 G7   C

carying havy load

     Fm7   G   Em7   A7

For the yoke I will give is easy and my burden is lightDm7

G7sus4   G7   C

Come to me and I Will give you rest....

Verse: do the same 1st verse:

when you feel the world is tumbling down on you

and you have no one that you can hold on to

Just face the rising sun and you'll see hope,

there's no need to run

Lift up your hands to God

And he'll make you feel alright....

Repeat Chorus

Where Filipinos are there you will find faith. There is no doubt that the Filipinos are able to smile in whatever time and situation because of many reasons as we have said earlier but the major reason is faith in God. Wherever Filipinos are there you will find God. Life is meaningless in the Philippines without God. We do not say all of them go to church everyday, no, but deep into their lives one finds a big space given to the power from above (God).

Go to every street even where there is no school, but one will find a chapel where Catholics are or a Mosque in Muslim areas. Go to the bank or industry, you will find a chapel or a schedule for mass. Join a graduation ceremony, prayer will start before anything else. Investors coming to the Philippines know this value, they allow them to have access for prayers especially on the first Friday of the month which is dedicated to the sacred heart of Jesus. Go to Malls, you will find a schedule for masses there. Go to schools and ask if there is any time to pray, definitely you will be told YES. Whatever house you enter try to look around, you will see either a statue of Mary, Sta Nino or any religious item placed in an open space. Filipinos carry this value to where ever they go even to

a communist or to the so called well developed countries. Meet the Filipino community, see them on Sundays where they go, for sure TO CHURCH. Where a Filipino is there the Church will be present. Mind you this is not one to one Filipino but the majority of Filipinos are **TEOPHILOS (Lovers of God)**.

Whatever county we come from indeed we have a lesson to learn from the Philippines. At times we said "If we were God, there could be no typhoon, earthquakes , floods, wars in the Philippines" but let God be called God and gold is tested to verify its goodness and its quality.

2. Proverbs 17:3 'Gold and silver are tested by fire, and a person's heart is tested by the Lord.'

3. 1Peter 1: 6-8 In this you rejoice, although now for a little while you may have to suffer through various trials, 7so that the genuineness of your faith, more precious than gold that is perishable even though tested by fire, may prove to be for praise, glory, and honor at the revelation of Jesus Christ.8Although you have not seen him you love him; even though you do not see him now yet believe in him, you rejoice with an indescribable and glorious joy9

Another reading we may find comes from the books of Sirach.

4. Sirach 2:1-11 My child, when you come to serve the Lord, prepare yourself for trials.

Be sincere of heart and steadfast,

and do not be impetuous in time of adversity.

Cling to him, do not leave him,

that you may prosper in your last days.

Accept whatever happens to you;

in periods of humiliation be patient.

For in fire gold is tested,

and the chosen, in the crucible of humiliation.

Trust in God, and he will help you;

make your ways straight and hope in him.

You that fear the Lord, wait for his mercy,

do not stray lest you fall.

You that fear the Lord, trust in him,

and your reward will not be lost.

You that fear the Lord, hope for good things,

for lasting joy and mercy.

Consider the generations long past and see:

has anyone trusted in the Lord and been disappointed?

Has anyone persevered in his fear and been forsaken?

has anyone called upon him and been ignored?

For the Lord is compassionate and merciful;

forgives sins and saves in time of trouble" In Summary the Bible teaches them to hope for tomorrow every time and that it is through sufferings that one can be seen as strong. 'Ang pagantus maghatag ug santos' It is throng suffering that one can become a saint'

SMILE IN THE FILIPINO PROFESSIONALISM.

A Profession is an occupation that aims at providing service to the community following an accumulated skills, knowledge and wisdom as fundamental values. Calgren (1999) Defines professionalism as an occupation that has crucial function in society and in which the exercise requires knowledge and skill and is bound by code of ethics. Professionalism differs from occupation. An occupation is any activity that a person is engaged while professionalism involves instrumental values, which guide behavior such as honesty and punctuality. It is the quality required or expected of members of a given profession possessing great skills and ability. Profession involves qualifications and performance standards of work/service. Characteristics of professionalism include: Skills and knowledge, accountability, competence, ethics, reliability, honesty, **respect, courtesy**, commitment and communication. The underlined words above say a lot about the Filipino life and work. According to Ken Alexander (Professionalism with a Smile). Patients entering an office for the first visit want to be reassured that they are in the right place. They tend to ask if that would be the right place to comfort them and get the quality service they need professionally. Ken says that even if professionalism involves many things, there is no way we can omit courtesy. "The **customer is a person who deserves to be treated with kindness, consideration and patience, no matter what the circumstances**" Ken Alexander recommends.

Ken says, Courtesy begins with a smile and treating patients or clients as if they are our guest at our homes. A smile is like sugar in ice cream. We can also say a smile is like salt added to food. One can add all the necessary ingredients but if he/she forgets to add salt, that will be a big lack on a taste, isn't it?

There is no greater universal sign that you care about a person and are willing to build a relationship with them than a good, old fashioned smile, people say. Professionalism needs a good face with hope. Besides, what does it cost to smile? Have you ever considered that the cost of a smile is not in what it takes you to produce it, but rather what it costs you when you do not smile regularly and often, you chase away customers indeed. **Many companies and countries including Tanzania (the writer's home country) are complaining of having few visitors. There are many factors involved in it but they need to ask if those who are assigned at the receptions and immigration can afford to smile a little.** People say, the first impression is very important. The airport probably can be one of the best airport constructed in the world, but that is not enough. Time may come when visitors get away from a certain country, those well constructed airports can remain achieves before the time due to lack of professionals working there without a smile. One would wonder flights landing daily on the so called one of 'the worst airports in the world' leaving behind the well constructed empty, why? SMILE.

The world is witnessing a multitude of Filipino workers working abroad, some are not learned so well than those from the developed countries. The world sees Asian work almost everywhere, if no Chinese is around a Filipino is present. One of the things one can ask is like why is it so? This book has already given an answer to this but a happy face says a lot. Working with joy and happy face makes a totality of goodness, it also makes the Client feel good and at home. Happy face hides challenges. A happy face allows challenges around the working place to open a door to solutions, because they give hope and courage. This is the point which calls Professionals to imitate, **working with hope to solve challenges.** Think, which company would like to have workers without hope? Workers who collapse after hearing problem? Which business operates without hope for the future? This is the point to keep on repeating. In the field of Professionalism, **hope**. There are two characteristics which matter so much: Honesty and confidentiality, but also there are others. Persons character often determine how successful they are in any career. People do not see one's inside, but what is expressed outside says a lot on how one could perform his/her duties and responsibilities.

The world if filled with Filipino, people say. In 2017 report from the Philippine government shows that at least there are between 9 to 12 million Filipino were outside their country. Can we learn from them? One of the things one can ask is like what is the secret behind? Indeed the secretes are already mentioned, which including hardworking people but we can not deny a SMILE which we mentioned as a component of happy face. Working with a smile make one feel good but also makes the Client feel comfortable. After seeing this one may conclude that, apart from employing them for different reasons, indeed a PINOY/PINAY SMILE says a lot to different companies in the world. The PINOY smile gives power to the interviewers for jobs worldwide. This is the power which gives them opportunity to fly, to work and help their fellow country men. This is what we call **THE POWER OF FILIPINO SMILE!** The honesty face gives hope and sincere smile. An honest person is like a trusted neighbor and citizen. He/she says the truth, no stealing, no cheating or use of fraud or any other trickery to acquire anything of value. Honesty imposes an obligation on all professional but above all is a smiling face. Smile now to be employed, smile now to give life back life and to welcome people to your heart and your area of work.

BELOW, CREATION OF A BIG SMILE THROUGH

PROVIDING A BALANCED DIET TO CHILDREN.

ADVERTISING AND EDITORIAL
E-MAIL : BUSINESSWEEKMINDANAO@GMAIL.COM
CONTACT NOS. : 0917-7121424 • 0947-8935776

MONDAY | JULY 18, 2016

FEATURE

BUSINESS WEEK 9
MINDANAO

Nutrition Month Feature:

DepEd 10 experience indicates CCTs key to improving malnourished school children's health

By MIKE BAÑOS

THERE appears to be a direct correlation between the improvement in school children's health and nutritional status and the Conditional Cash Transfers (CCTs) their families have been receiving under the government's Pantawid Pamilyang Pilipino Program (4Ps).

Department of Education Region X Dir. Allan G. Farnazo said because parents, especially the mothers, of students classified as malnourished or severely wasted, have been closely monitoring their children's attendance in school, the school attendance has increased tremendously, and as a result, these children have been successfully reached by the agency's supplemental feeding program.

"We noticed the mothers are very involved in the program," Farnazo said. "If you call their attention about their children's absences, they become worried it would remove them from the program. As a result, when students are physically present in school, natututukan ang kanilang nutrition kaya nag-improve."

Jeff M. Rona, a nutritionist/dietician consultant charged with DepEd-10's supplemental feeding program, said figures on the children's individual nutrition status, height and weight have shown a marked improvement over the past years the program has been implemented.

From School Year (SY) 2010-2011 to SY 2014-2015, DepEd-10 records for elementary school children in

wasted children declining 68% from 16,187 to 5,240; wasted children declined 15% from 53,352 to 20,468; overweight children decreased 67% from 10,966 to 3,609 and obese children declined 63% from 1,908 to 698.

Since the 4Ps program was implemented, Farnazo said the budget for the supplemental feeding program which covers 120 feeding days every school year has increased from PhP 25-million in 2012 to PhP168-M in 2016 and implementation transferred from the Department of Social Welfare & Development (DSWD) to the individual schools.

"So we captured the severely malnourished and severely wasted children in the schools and improved their nutritional status," Farnazo noted.

Although the supplemental feeding program is hobbled by budgetary constraints which still allocates a mere PhP18 per child for lunch, it has tremendously expanded its coverage and now covers more children with better meals made possible by technological improvements such as rice mongo blend and rice mongo crunchies developed by the Food and Nutrition Research

Technology (DOST). The CCTs, coupled with the supplemental feeding program and the strict implementation of the DepEd ban on the sale of soft drinks and junk foods in school canteens, all appear to have contributed to the marked improvement in school children's nutrition, attendance and academic performance. Further on, DepEd-10 would like to see enhancements in the program which is being administered by the Health and Nutrition Dept. of the DepEd Central Office in Manila. Although the regional offices can only make recommendations based on their experience on the ground, Farnazo believes they can still contribute significant improvements in this manner.

For instance, an improvement in the coverage and scope of supplemental feeding program for pre-school children aged 5 years old and below, would be a welcome step forward for the Early Child Care & Development (ECCD) of local government units down to the barangay level which are implementing it with DSWD in Day Care

This is strongly indicated in data from the Cagayan de Oro City Social Welfare and Development (CSWD) office which set its Supplementary Feeding Program as a priority thrust through the doubling of its fund allocation from PhP 9-million in 2013 to PhP 19-million in 2016 for the health and nutrition of children in Day Care Centers/Child Development Centers.

As a result, the number of severely underweight children under the program dropped 72.4% for the three-year period (from 118 to only 9); the underweight children count decreased 76% (from 756 to only 182), while the number of overweight children was reduced 27% (from 372 to 272). Consequently, the number of normal children monitored under the program increased by 2,300 or a 10% increase to 26,081.

Data from the Department of Social Welfare and Development Region

50% from 817 to 372; and the total number of malnourished kids dropped an impressive 55% from 8,122 to only 3,663 by the 5th cycle.

As a result, the incidence of malnutrition in the region declined from 8% to only 2.5%, while the total number of children rehabilitated increased 36% from 10,367 to 14,140 by the end of the 5th cycle; and the number of normal children increased 50% from 93,082 to 139,958.

now without a better alternative, we will constantly be going back to zero."

"I think we should continue the 4Ps, we just need to improve the implementing mechanism like who should benefit and who should be excluded." Farnazo said, "Effects are better felt compared to earlier when there were none."

However, he notes the general perception that the schools can do it all is a real

Fr Adam Joe Bago Cssp trained parents in Digkilaan Parish in hills of Iligan to mix rice with coconut milk for a cheap but nutritious meal. He is DepEd's ALS coordinator for the area.

BIBLIOGRAPHY.

www.reflect-action.org

https://www.pinoymoneytalk.com/ofw-population-country-age-

sex-work-type/

www.plosmedicine.org/article/info:doi/10.1371/journal.pmed.

1000363

Overseas Filipino Workers (OFW): Demographic Data

www.unesco.org/uil/htbade/

(http://online.sfsu.edu/rone/Buddhism/footsteps.htm)
https://quizlet.com/621623/spa

nish-numbers-1-20-flash-cards/

Speaking Cebuano, Pronunciation and Dialogues
by Maryknoll Institute of Language and Culture,
Davao City, 1999

Cebuano Particles and Word List, Davao City, 1995).

www.thefreedictionary.com
http://idiomaticexpressions.org/

https://quizlet.com/621623/spanish-numbers-1-20-flash-cards/

www.thefreedictionary.com
http://idiomaticexpressions.org/
https://careertrend.com

Josephsonbusnessethics.com

"Philippines - Language, Culture, Customs and

Etiquette."   Kwintessential.

http://www.kwintessential.co.uk/resources/global-

etiquette/philippines-country-profile.html

(accessed on 6 November 2007) "Alternative Concepts and Other
Values   of   the   Filipinos."   Livinginthephilippines.
http://www.livinginthephilippines.com/philculture/alternativ
e.html   (accessed   6   November   2007)
http://www.unesco.org/uil/litbase/?menu=9&program=16

Monaghan, John and Just, Peter (2000).

 SocialandCultural Anthropology: A VeryShortIntroduction.
Oxford University Press.

Philippine Constitution (1987)

Quito, Emerito S. "The Ambivalence of Filipino Traits and Values." Cultural Heritage and Contemporary Change. http://www.crvp.org/book/Series03/III-7/chapter_v.htm (accessed 14 November 2007)

Gorospe, Vitaliano R., S.J. "Understanding the Filipino Value System." http://www.crvp.org/book/Series03/III-7/chapter_vi.htm (accessed 14 November 2007)

Notes: *Informal Education is a general term for education that occurs outside of a structured curriculum. This is the education which makes a person experience and make changes. This form of learning makes us humble enough to respect others including those who have not gone to school at all. It makes us say, 'so there is big knowledge outside the classroom too!' This is where one bridges the gape between school and life and touch the real life. This is where an interaction is taking place. Therefore, this work was a proof that there are is a lot we can learn from outside people which can make us live better than yesterday.*

www.ingramcontent.com/pod-product-compliance
Lightning Source LLC
Chambersburg PA
CBHW060702030426
42337CB00017B/2722